D0622586

DATE DUE

WITHDRAWN

DEMCO

The American Book of the Dead

BOOKS BY JIM BARNES

The Fish on Poteau Mountain (poems)
Summons and Sign: Poems by Dagmar Nick
This Crazy Land (poems)

The American Book of the Dead

Poems by Jim Barnes

For Jerry, brother in the blood, met once again in California — Let us not forget our responsibilities — ch'i hana hilia,

Jim Barnes

4-20-89

University of Illinois Press
Urbana / Chicago / London

Grateful acknowledgment is made to the National Endowment for the Arts
for a writing fellowship which made the completion of many of these poems
possible.

Publication of this work was supported in part by grants from the Illinois Arts
Council (a state agency) and the National Endowment for the Arts.

A portion of the section entitled "This Crazy Land" appeared in the chapbook
This Crazy Land (Tempe, Arizona: Inland Boat Series/*Porch* Publications,
1980), copyright © 1980 by Jim Barnes.

The poems "Return to La Plata, Missouri," "Elegy for the Girl Who Drowned
at Goats Bluff," "Postcard to Grace Schulman" (under the title "Letter to a
Poet"), "Autobiography, Chapter XVII: Floating the Big Piney," "Autobiography,
Chapter VI: San Diego Harbor at Dusk," "The Last Chance," "Midwest
Midwinter" (under the title "Midwinter") appeared in *The Nation,* copyright
© 1975, 1976, 1977, 1978 by *The Nation.*

Library of Congress Cataloging in Publication Data

Barnes, Jim, 1933–
The American book of the dead.

I. Title.
PS3552.A67395A8   811'.54   81–11458
ISBN 0–252–00937–1 (cloth)   AACR2
ISBN 0–252–00938–x (paper)

Many of the poems in this volume first appeared in
the following publications, to whose editors grateful acknowledgment
is made for permission to reprint:

Invisible City: "Autobiography, Chapter I: Leaving Summerfield"

Shantih: "The Chicago Odyssey," "Year's End 1977"

Poem: "On the Beach at Manzanita, Oregon"

Long Pond Review: "Autobiographical Flashback: Puma and Pokeweed," "On the
Bridge at Fourche Maline River"

El Nahuatzen: "These Mysteries"

Northwest Review: "Last Look at La Plata, Missouri"

The Nation: "Return to La Plata, Missouri," "Elegy for the Girl Who Drowned
at Goats Bluff," "Postcard to Grace Schulman," "Autobiography, Chapter
XVII: Floating the Big Piney," "Autobiography, Chapter VI: San Diego Harbor
at Dusk," "The Last Chance," "Midwest Midwinter"

The New Mexico Humanities Review: "An ex-Deputy Sheriff Remembers the
Eastern Oklahoma Murderers"

Quarry West: "Autobiography, Chapter VII: Home for Memorial Day,"
"The Exact Center of the World"

Slackwater Review: "Sundown at Swan Lake, Missouri" (under the title "Sundown
at Lake Tenkiller"), "Autobiography, Chapter VIII: At the Sand Fields"

The Chicago Review: "The Body Falters," "Pyramid Lake, Late Summer,"
"Still-Hildreth Sanitarium: Ice Fishing" (under the title "Sanitarium Lake:
Ice Fishing"), "Lost in Sulphur Canyons"

Separate Doors: "On the Eve of My Parents' Sixtieth Anniversary"

New Letters: "Old Soldiers' Home at Marshalltown, Iowa"

Green River Review: "Swan Lake, Again"

Colorado North Review: "For a Drowned Sailor, Age 4"

Poetry Northwest: "Scouting Tom Fry Hollow," "Against Metempsychosis &c."

Images: "On Top of Winding Stair Mountain"

Poetry Now: "Under Buffalo Mountain"

Quarterly West: "Autobiography, Chapter XIV: Tombstone at Petit Bay,
Near Tahlequah," "San Miguel de Allende," "Autobiography, Chapter XIX:
For Andrew Grossbardt, in Memoriam"

Wanbli Ho: "Tracking the Siuslaw Man"

Wind: "The Last Trip Somewhere West"

The Magic of Names: "Autobiography, Chapter XVI: Return to Rich Mountain"

The Seattle Review: "Comcomly's Skull"

Outer Bridge: "The Only Photograph of Quentin at Harvard," "Autobiography,
Chapter XIII: Ghost Train, the Dream"

The Missouri Review: "My Father's House," "Memoirs of a Catskinner"

The Denver Quarterly: "Autobiography, Chapter XII: Hearing Montana"

Wisconsin Review: "In Rudolph's Cave"

The Mississippi Mud: "Dog Days 1978," "Loving the Distant Nude"

CutBank: "Autobiography, Chapter IX: Leaving, Again," "Autobiography, Chapter XI: Prelude to Writing," "Autobiography, Chapter IV: The Mirage"

Practices of the Wind: "Winter Pastoral"

Mississippi Valley Review: "Contemporary Native American Poetry"

Phantasm: "Autobiography, Chapter II: Setting Out," "Autobiography, Chapter XLII: Three Days in Louisville"

New America: A Review: "Wild Horse Hollow"

South Dakota Review: "Autobiography, Chapter V: Ghost Town"

Greenfield Review: "Tornado"

New River Review: "Stopping on Kiamichi Mountain"

Panache: "Autobiography: Last Chapter"

Contents

III. Ishmael

IV. Night Falls, Ritual and Fast

The American Book of the Dead

To be rolled up the size of a small god's scroll,
to be placed in the journeyer's good right hand,
to be, as it were, an extra finger

> *touching the stilled heart,*
> *requesting voice.*

To have been written by a company of good poets,
to have been judged a map of the right way,
to have been perceived at the moment of passing

> *by the voyager at the gate.*

So that the words not ring hollow
down the corridors of doom or dome,

> *let the last little book*

be of softest vellum, only a whispering skin,
that may fade as the body fades

> *before Eridanus or the Po.*

Let us all carry into death the words we could not,
lifebound, bear and in whatever other worlds

> *say them unafraid.*

I
This Crazy Land

Henry lay in de netting, wild,
while the brainfever bird did scales;
Mr. Heartbreak, the New Man,
come to farm a crazy land;
an image of the dead on the fingernail
of a newborn child.

JOHN BERRYMAN
"Dream Song 5"

Autobiography, Chapter I: Leaving Summerfield

Low wind across old weeds warps your sense of hours;
the day is heavy with cloud and slow hawks.

The last false-front you catch sight of cracks
the color of old harness, rattles like bone
chimes in a wind you know you will never
see clear through.

The road straight out is black with tar oozed
into itself; fenced against the road, the weeds
wait out the wire.

The sun has danced upon this town and gone; not
even a mirage is left to lie you lives you
sometimes thought you'd live.

There's a distant sound of bells you know don't ring.

The last false-front is falling with your years;
your eyes are webbing with the panes.

You curse the damned town for all you're worth,
but know you'll have to come home again,
fast as a rabid fox, when the years have made
the town quick with old men's dream.

The Chicago Odyssey

Looking north you try to break through the sky
with your bad eyes. You want to map the town.
The lake and leaden sky are one, a blank
canvas on which you'd like to sketch a face.
The artist in you tells you to wait for dream.
You wait and nothing comes. You try museums,
their rigid worth, view mummies and other
wonders hardly half as strange as this place,
this time. A gauze of snow spirals up your spine.
You tell yourself the ice age now begins
and you alone must escape to tell the tale:
the horror of his and hers fleshed in frost,
the scream caught suddenly in mid-flight,
the running child quick-frozen in the park,
towers icicled in reverse, the el turned
easy slope for otters.

                    All as the world turns
the other way. You turn and traffic whirs.
The astronomy is wrong: there are no stars,
moon breaks crystalline, the only zodiac
is flake on flake, a kaleidoscope of air.
You swore you'd know this town and now you don't.
Something has tipped the day and up is down;
you're trying your best to leave while there's still
a time. From each corner comes a siren's song.
Every street's a cliff you tack away from,
cotton in your ears against the damning wind
you never thought could be so cold, so insistent
on its icy trade, that barter would mean

the loss of teeth. You'll suck your eyes back in
your head, lean hard into the coming night,
lie always, go native, and by God survive.

On the Beach at Manzanita, Oregon

for Tom and Chris, Choctaw and Yuchi

Over my shoulder Neahkanie Mountain
parts the wind and clouds headed for Bend,
and here stands a stone marked by unknown hands:
two centuries' scribbling on this salt sea stone.
Clatsop, Spaniard, local loggers' marks?
Big Tree says his people used to dig up beeswax
by tons at Nehalem Spit to trade for glass
when the land was young and sea was hard for ships.
The cryptic stone faces seaward, its secret
kept: townsfolk say a hoard of gold lies buried
beneath the sand, just under the mountain's eye.
But buried is not the word:

                    Listen to the wind,
hear the dip of oars in waves the Clatsop braved
to look for smelt or beeswax on the beach,
remember the man who breathed salt air and spruce
who too once stood on this smooth plot of earth.

Time ebbs, ebbs for me as I stand beside
the hallowed stone and think of steelhead running
and Spanish bones down deep out there and sift
the black granite sand through my fingers here
while the ageless Chinook works its warm way through
the tunnels in my mind.

                    A dying race,
the Yuchis of Oklahoma can count but few
of their tribe alive. Drowned Phoenician sailors.
In our adopted land when Chief and I

6

were twelve or so, we rode the prairies west,
west and back again, bareback and double
astride the fast bay mare our fathers had.
Once we could not hold on and plunged headlong
into the rolling waves of wind on sage
while the bay coursed on across horizons red
with Yuchi paint.

          The sounds of sea strike deep
the chords of memory. The stone stands silent,
immense in its place on this northern strand.

Autobiographical Flashback: Puma and Pokeweed

I've spoken of home before and spotted crows
older than my hair. I generalize: home
is where hard is. And know it true. The crow
is constant color: his caw can crack a stone.

You keep your crows alive as best you can:
you remember a puma and pokeweed and trees
quick with wings and wind, tell yourself the fear
you felt along your fingertips would freeze

your sanity now, if you were child again,
free to feel again leaves upon your head,
to break off shoots of poke for suppertime,
to dream the cry of a puma one time heard.

Your memory is rocked by things you have
neglected; your stoned eyes are hard with world
you are late to see. And even now you know
the facts are wrong, as random and whorled

as fingerprints on records you've tried to keep
or the circling crows that blot your inland sky.

Still-Hildreth Sanitarium: Fishing

You come here when there's nothing else to do:
the kids in school, the wife working ten to
four, you off for months you don't care to count.
The sanitarium stands as empty as your head
must be to know the place in full. The flood
of bathing ghosts around the private lake
takes your mind, wave after wave, until you
drown in things you can never really know,
but think you can.

           The cracking skylight three
stories above your head is bound to fall
upon the ballroom floor where other ghosts
know no end to dance and music forever
spiels. You could go mad here except for needs.
The bass you plan to take from the darker side
of the lake were spawned when the grounds
were rich from insanity. But you are sane,
the water is sane, the day is sane.

                 You know
this sanctuary Van Johnson chose to dry out in
is a marvel you can never reckon with.
Why it failed had something to do with dollars
and decay. Upkeep and appearance were
vital as the light it took for Van
to see the light. Windows crack under your
eyes. Even ghosts are drowning in current dance.
You fish for bass and contemplate the end.

These Mysteries

Walking these hills
you have a sense
of distance:

each stone
a mystery
in relation
to all others.

The space between
is question.

Then
the unnatural
shape
marks earth:

a sharp wonder.

Obsidian chipped
so perfect
the sky's a lie.

Hand and eye
you try
the black edges:

the minuscule contours
of hill, hollow,
the semblance
of a dead sea.

A ghost
in your bones
begins a dance,
a rhythm of blood
you cannot name.

These hills
where the hawk
is silent,

these hills
where the crow
has forgotten the caw,

these hills,
these mysteries,
cloud your eyes
as earth
the agate.

You want to know
the secret of stone,
the vision
that pounds your skull.

The sky will not yield:
the day drums down.

Last Look at La Plata, Missouri

The park, the heart, you see at town's center is soft
underfoot. All winter long the dying bluegrass
has fed on cicada bones, enough to fill a loft:

the drone of dying, constant cymbals and hard bass,
recedes to a waning echo in your ear. Each year
the town drops an inch or two in the mud, and has

little sense of its going, though a certain fear
of losing trade caused The Palace to buy a shade
and paint the yellow Open sign and sell kids beer.

The town speaks of history, and goes slightly mad.
The silver jet, the town's only hero's joke it's said,
has lost a tire; the fuselage and wing tanks, glad

for past skies, are captive to flung rocks and love-red
names. Summer was too long and heavy for the white
bandstand warping above lost chords and maidenheads.

The town affirms its past. The druggist kills his light
above the store. A diesel moans toward Kansas City.
A lone dog barks. A child cries. All of a winter night.

Return to La Plata, Missouri

The warping bandstand reminds you of the hard rage
you felt in the heart of the town the day you said goodbye
to the park, silver jet, and cicadas dead in the sage.

The town is basic red, although it browns. A cry
of murder, rape, or wrong will always bend the night
hard into the broken grass. You listen close for sighs

of lovers on the ground. The darkness gathers light
and throws it down: something glows that you cannot name,
something fierce, abstract, given time and space you might

on a journey leave behind, a stone to carve your fame
on, or a simple word like *love*. The sun is down
or always going down in La Plata, the same

sun. Same too the child's cry that turns the mother's frown
brittle as chalk or the town's face against the moon.
Same too the moan of dog and diesel circling the town

in an air so heavy with cloud that there is little room
for breath or moon. Strange: in a town so country, so
foreign, you never hear a song nor see a loom

pattern dark threads into a history you would know
and would not know. You think you see one silver star.
But the town offers only itself, and you must go.

An ex-Deputy Sheriff Remembers
the Eastern Oklahoma Murderers

i. Summerfield

They took a tire tool to his head,
this gentle stranger from Wyoming.
Oh, we caught them over
at Talihina drinking beer
at Lester's Place, calling
the myna bird bad names
and shooting shuffleboard.
I'm telling you
they were meek in the muzzle
of our guns. They claimed innocence
and: why, they went fishing
with the Cowboy just the other day.
We said we knew, knew too
the way they stole him blind
that night. We spoke of blood,
the way the dogs had lapped his face.
The youngest of the three bad brothers,
barely thirteen, began to cry:
"He told us everything was all right
and we hit him till he died."
And that is how it was,
a simple thing, like breathing,
they hit him until he died,
until he bled Wyoming dry
there on the road
in that part of Oklahoma
no stranger has ever owned.

We shot the Choctaw way back in '94,
last legal execution by firing squad.
He didn't die, through the heart, square
and he didn't die.
The high sheriff, my old boss,
stuffed his own shirt down
the Choctaw's neck
to stop the rattle in his throat.
You couldn't shoot a downed man
no matter what and he had to die.
Damned good Choctaw, I'll say that.
Red Oak had no jail and it was too
blasted cruel to execute him
before his crop was in. The judge
scheduled it for the fall, first Saturday
after the corn was in the Choctaw's crib.
That damned fool Choctaw gathered
his corn like any other dirt farmer,
dressed clean, and kept his word.
"I'm ready" is all he said that day.
You got to admire a man like that,
Indian or not, murderer or just plain fool.
He'd shot three men for sleeping
in his barn and taking the milk bucket
away from his little girl, though she
wasn't harmed at all, and he showed up
just like he'd said he would.

                        There
was a picnic in the shade after we choked
the Choctaw to death and took the rifle home.
First time I'd ever seen a camera,
big damned black thing on legs,

smelled like seven kinds of sin every time
it popped. Had fresh hominy and chicken and the last
of some damned fine late sweet red watermelons.

iii. LeFlore

Goddamnest thing I ever saw
was when old Mac ran down that poor old LeFlore boy.
Old Mac was drunk as thunder
when we chained him to the tree
he'd just pissed on back of his house.
Said he'd wanted to see what it was like
to bounce a man off the hood
of the truck he hauled pulpwood on.
No other reason than just that.
Hell of a note, but I've heard worse.
They all have got some sort of song and dance.
Old Mac's kids were screaming louder
than the crows and threatening us with garden hoes.
We shooed them off with fake fast draws.
That poor old LeFlore boy was as deaf as stone,
a condition they say came with the color of his skin,
though as mild in his ways as the first fall winds.
Old Mac had hit him from behind. Coming
down the gravel road, lord, he must have been
doing sixty and with a full two-cord load.
Hit him dead on. Center. Cracked his
back in half all the way through. That poor
old LeFlore boy's rubber boots were left
standing exactly where he last had stood.
How can you account for that, those silly
rubber boots standing bolt upright
dead in the middle of the goddamned road?

iv. Wister

What made him think he could get away with it
is beyond me. Hell, he'd lived over at Glendale
all his life. Everybody knew he had a stiff
little finger on his right hand. The mask hid
nothing, not even the fear and tobacco juice
he always drooled out the corners of his mouth.
He shot the teller right between the eyes and
made the others strip. Don't ask why. Cleaned
out the vault of a thousand dollars, mostly
fives, and made it fifty yards down the Frisco
tracks before Mathes, the bank's owner, naked
as a jaybird and pissing a blue streak, blew
his left shoulder off with a 30.06. I've got
the cartridge shell to this day. Was going to
have one of them little lighters, size of your
finger, made out of it. But I decided to quit.

Autobiography, Chapter VII:
Home for Memorial Day

The names that trust their bones to this hot hill
    have learned the rage of stone and pine. The wind
    that brings the morning into your eyes says live.
    You try a stone, find it rooted past your years.
    You question why you came. The answer comes out
    wrong as the women you haven't seen since hot sin
    was in your groin. Belovéd, Gone From This World,
    in weeds. Gold in a mourner's teeth names you fool.

Years past they used to spread a picnic under pines,
    sing hymns that sparked a bright beyond, and lovers
    rolled on stones and needles fierce to skin. You feel
    yourself in somebody else's dream: one friend whose
    hello is too far away to see, relatives too golden to
    touch, the *Requiescat In Pace* no foreigner can read.

You tell the fat friend you no longer know your life
    and see your epitaph in his handful of white roses.
    The way he hides his flowers behind somebody's name
    makes you feel the shame. His Belovéd cannot be read
    because of weeds. You want to touch his stone, tell
    him: we have endured. But you say something vague—
    yesterday's weather, God—customary words to exit on.

II
Death by Water

In the after-death state the deceased imagines that he has a physical body, though he has been severed therefrom by the high surgery of death.

SIR JOHN WOODROFFE
in an introduction to the
Tibetan Book of the Dead

Sundown at Swan Lake, Missouri

At the lake's edge
I face the west
and count
last waves
dying in the sun.

The speedboats' rip
recedes
to the far edge
of my inner ear.
The wake vanishes.

Stones turn cold
beneath my feet.
The day falls
as fast as
a hawk to prey.

I do not want
to be anywhere
except here:
the waves
cease to break

and last birds
glide unruffled
at my feet
across the constant
plain of sky.

My eyes are full
of the silver
of water, a smooth
metal drawing
my hands

to the test
I refuse
to take:
I will not drown
to know my life.

The Body Falters

The forest thickens
my blood. I stumble
on acorns grown
the size of apples,
sticks no larger
than the gnat's eye.
I am animal
in this old darkness
I have not known
for years. The body
falters, the mind
joins the earth.
The sound of crawling
cracks my ears
and of the lively trees,
the brown, brown grass,
and the one voice
of the steady river.
I have never been
anywhere but here,
flat on my stomach
embracing the constant
earth, this world
I hold. Sky on my back
I feel the needled wheel
of stars tracking
my skin with pores
deep as moonlight.
My eyes break into
the earth, into
the dark alluvial

blood. Beyond
this place:
only another
and another
and another.
I am repeated
into the earth.

On the Eve of My Parents' Sixtieth Anniversary

I wake to the way:
the road stretches out
like a knotted thread,

the towns' eyes
I have to
live through.

Woven into
these hard lives
I know myself
by the pattern
of roads,

the tapestried earth,
the maze of ends.

I come bearing
the only gift
I have:

this handful
of loneliness,
sheared
like loose ends
from the clothes
of strangers.

Old Soldiers' Home at Marshalltown, Iowa

No movement on the hill: the old soldiers
are dying, dying into mushrooms they dream.
On the grounds near the rising river, the slow
phallic plants grow white and low. The days
swell, and no one stoops to the task at hand.

The old soldiers are dying, dying into the spring:
statues turn green with the grass. The tavern
at 13th and Summit echoes this green death,
but there is no song of esprit de corps,
no body lying on the floor drunk on
a reverie of a Flanders field or Argonne.

Even the drugstore across from the gate
is as vacant as the eyes you sometimes see
at the dark windows on the hill. The years
have emptied Seberg's of more than wares.
Time was when Jean Seberg was a bedside name,
the darling of bored veterans and gossips in
this town, the star of Saturday matinees.

From the tavern stool, you listen to the whir
of the laundromat across the street washing
some lonely nurse's whites, spinning them free
of trenches, the soiled touch she's come to dread.
You know that you've got it wrong, dead wrong,
that life here is as vital as your organs.
But somewhere in your head the old soldiers
are dying, dying into the fullness of spring.

Swan Lake, Again

I name this lake
a wash for tired eyes,

a balm for the poor
Galahad, the quester

I am for words.
There's something in

the blood that draws
the water to my eyes,

something that knows
the slightest of things

must be named.
Even the snake

down there, down there,
curling through my hair.

There are dreams
of water

snakes have
I can never know,

but when you
curl through me,

I feel my marrow twist,
old friend,

brother to my blood,
sworn enemy of heels.

Pyramid Lake, Late Summer

The stone shore
cracks with
the sinking years:

fissures fan out
and map the heavy sky,
the broken water,

even
write your name
in arabesques

you are afraid
to trace. An ancient fear
grooves your face.

At your back
somewhere, near,
the desert grows.

Beyond your eyes
the water strikes
the sky into waves.

You will leave
this place now,
but first

you will,
stone by stone, take
away your name.

For a Drowned Sailor, Age 4

Times
the drowned child
fades into your dream
of fish, you let
the line go slack
and try not to snag
the smallest limb.
Your arms sink.
Now, the news
he cannot be found
stays the rod. Death
by water, the loveliest
of deaths by far,
rainbows
you cannot dream.
Now into sundown
the mother sounds
for the lost child.
Though you no longer
see the boat, her face,
blank as the last dull
light, will not fade.
You no longer hear
her cry, hear only
a lowing
across the water,
like soft cannon,
a lowing
carrying miles
across the water.

Elegy for the Girl Who Drowned at Goats Bluff

The sun strikes water like soft stone,
oblique and torn by surface waves.
Below, in the still place of stone,
the slow fish nuzzle through the caves

you seldom know are there at all
and rest among the drowned girl's bones.
Above, the bluff is too brittle
for a date in stone. The long day downs,

and she alone records the passing.
You think you know her now, the scream
that cracked the bluff, the siren song
that wails its way into the dream

you sometimes have. Dark water.
Darker still the night. You wait
for the water to take the sky, for
the floating moon to turn stone white

as the skin of dead fish. You know
she sees you stranger to this place,
her empty eyes wide against the night,
her empty hands, her empty face.

Postcard to Grace Schulman

Here in this fireplace the flame dies into
ash and the night closes in, gray, winged:
a silent, deadly air as heavy as old snow.
I must write you, now, that your felt presence
is enough, that the stilling voice of your poems
goes the way of fire, consumes, and is done,
that the voice sings through wood, andiron, attic
flue, and what's left is the heavy weight of ash,
an old snow for old men to worship in.
Clothed in this mourning air, I kneel here to
find one coal, one burning wing of light,
an affirmation. Something as inexplicable
as words has risen through my open hands.

Autobiography, Chapter XVII: Floating the Big Piney

How the river cools your blood is something you can't
    explain: you search the bottom stones for words
    unscientific, words fleshed with the sound of sense,
    maybe a chant laid upon the water the time
    words were all and fathers sang their sons ways
    to be and the river flowed sure of its pace.

You lie back in the canoe. Your own child points the bow
    now into the blue breath of sky: trees course
    overhead, and your eyes bend with pillars
    of air, the cornering birds; you lie back into
    the dream you know you'll have just once, a token
    from a far time, a river you can't explain.

All words are lost and you want to sing the meaning
    and origin of things, to make an appositive
    of light, something solid as a stone to hand
    this man-child. But all you have to offer is
    pause, the silence of water and the small
    knowledge that the river takes you over all.

Scouting Tom Fry Hollow

The trail in I blazed on pine is gone
without a trace. The lay of the land and sky
has run amuck. I check the ridge south,
look for marks I know cannot be there now.

One thing remains unchanged. The hollow hard
below: the brown, brown grass flowing around
chimney rubble and collapsed corral, the sound
of distant wolves keening in the stony hills.

I go down, as before, to look for the grave
I will not find again. The wind always
blows and sundown comes hours ahead of time.
Little chance any artifact is left

to clear the name of bones the hollow bears.
Grave unmarked, the hanged man still hangs under
the ghost of every tree. I raise a stone,
poor homage, for the next man to wonder on.

On Top of Winding Stair Mountain

Halfway done with this mountain,
I stuff wild berries into my mouth
like a starving coon chased to bone.
As far as I can see is blue.
I swallow the space of valleys
and grow drunk with the vision
that blues my eyes. I feel
my lips, my tongue, my throat
assuming the color of air.
Shadows nest in my ears.

High on this mountain, my hands
are scarred from feathers or fear
I would give lives to remember.
I reach for the sun, crazy with
the moment, and somewhere there
is an echo of a crash, a sound
of broken water, a far cry
through silence. My legs are stone
as bedrock. I turn back, hand
and mouth, to berries as a lone
hawk plummets into the world.

Under Buffalo Mountain

The prairie flows toward
the sacred lake

where the silent water
waits, deep

in its secret of geese,
for the coming of snow.

Here the Choctaw stopped, forever,
staked the ground

with bones broken beyond rage.
Blood hides

in these hills and haunts
the faded town:

the drunk drowns in sleep,
the geese forget to come,

the snow falls,
and the moon is down.

Autobiography, Chapter XIV:
Tombstone at Petit Bay, Near Tahlequah*

Looking for artifacts that map your world less real,
    you find the obelisk, dwarfed among the weeds;
    knee-high and almost growing from the chert
    hillside, it hides its legend like night the
    features of a face.

You read the date, 1839. And the one faint vertical
    word, *child*, in Sikwayi script. The grave where
    no grave should be gently shocks your senses
    clean: each fracture of chert is bone. You feel
    a sudden reverence for all stone.

Years you've quested in these hills, a running search
    for something still you cannot name—something
    holy, proof of migration or lost Phoenician sailors.

You are tempted toward a gentle excavation, but know
    you will not dig into the earth for the same
    reason you never move the soil except to plant.

The obelisk casts a shadow longer than its length.
    The narrow darkness leans along the hill, toward
    the bay and the slow moon rising from the fabled
    east.

*Tahlequah, capital of the Cherokee Nation; also reputed to mean
"one got lost."

Still-Hildreth Sanitarium: Ice Fishing

Huddled like a lost child round his knees,
I cover the hole I hacked in the ice.
Like an idiot I would know the secret
of fish. Here in the middle of the solid
lake, the fish I take are pale with
the cold fever of winter, their scales
shocked at 5 below into fast freeze.

The sanitarium at my back is dead
against the frozen sky. I try
to visualize a sun, one to burn
my head clear of ice, clear of broken
glass and the footless shoe I saw
last fall where the lilies now lie dead.
Cold this lake has always been: cold then
with swimmers numbed by electric shock,
cold now from arctic ice, from window
panes sucked down by a force I cannot
read, from ghosts wandering on the hill.

To come here in dead of winter
is to die or know the quality of ice.
You have to watch your mind. I still
can see the agony and the pain
plain on many a face that ever
did time here. But tell yourself: given
another life, you could have lost
your sins here. The sky is blank,
will stay blank until the season shocks
itself sensible again, until the fish
no longer freeze in the hook of my hand.

On the horizon, stars break through the fog; below the hotel,
    the *Star of India* lists against the pier under a growing
    heaviness of spent lives.

The steel hull strains under the thunder of the distant seas,
    the harsh light of the shore, the broken wind fit for
    no sail.

The masts and beams turn salt with the barnacle years: the ship
    waits for the fullness of dark and one last voyage down
    the other side of the sky, one last captain, one last crew,
    and the last of pilgrims wanting only the openness of sea.

The harbor grows with the dusk, and ghosts ride the tide and
    town,
    immigrant souls wandering the foreign edge waiting for the
    passage that will not come.

For these souls this poem, poor payment for what I cannot give:
    a promise of sails. For this is no hell and I no master
    of ships.

Tracking the Siuslaw Man

for Lethe Easterling

Ice honed by wind
is sharp with messages from the north.
Firs split under silver blades,
and tracks are fossils under glass.

You read the rigid trail
under a sun dead as amber,
tell yourself the cold you feel
can't touch the fear

in the marrow of your bones.
Siuslaw passed this way is what you know
from footprints hairy with frost
and shadows in the wood that will not freeze.

The trail always ends
on solid stone mute with glyphs
that send you back centuries
or into a dream you never want to have.

You hack the last print
from the glazed ground, feel it shatter
in your hand while somewhere
a dark Siuslaw raven calls

and snow men bend to the task of mountains.

San Miguel de Allende

In San Miguel de Allende
you count the stars by twos.

Even the moon's a lover,
Mars at her lips.

A sagging Mary hangs on the wall
with her stone Jesus.

Nobody's ever alone
in this place of echoes.

Once in a rare sundown
we saw the clouds twice catch fire,

one sun trailing the other down
like a red pariah dog.

The Last Trip Somewhere West

On the freeway,
heading west,

I run through
miles of sun,

the road behind
passing away

like the light,
until the sun

beats me down,
stands dead still

west of me,
then drops below

the day's last edge.
I bury

my eyes
in the night

and drive toward
the road's end.

Autobiography, Chapter XVI: Return to Rich Mountain

This is the spot where you killed yourself with bad gin,
    the phony suicide you thought would work.
    That's past, and you'd like to say you've grown
    new feet to grip this everlasting earth.
    No, you're no lizard that in losing a leg
    grows another newer, better than before.

Ghosts and prophecies flood your mind, but you're no saint.
    You proved it then, and now you'll never brag
    you held the day or ever stopped the sun
    while walls crumbled and the old queen's summer castle,
    now restored, sank into the dust. A long
    day of abdication in '48.
    Wilhelmina's long gone. God save the Queen.
    Her last stone castle runes this mountainside.

The only thing you've grown is a salty set of eyes.
    You see this pirated mountain earth alive
    with forebears, Indians gathering herbs for cure.
    You're blind to Sunday traffic from Little Rock,
    and the work you have to do to live and love,
    still another philosophy in stone.
    You come here to contemplate your only fame,
    a wandering Dutchman, world without an end.

This day is as wide and open as it ever was.
    The dark ascends, a vast sea of water,
    even before the sun goes down. You leave
    the hot cot and ask your legs to verify
    the sinking earth. Somewhere far off below

in the real land the sad twang of mandolins
tells you this is no foreign country now.
The pines are here, the needles in your hair.

Comcomly's Skull

Comcomly's skull is coming home.
That wily one-eyed Chinook chief,
whose other bones are scattered from
the grave, keeper of slaves, thief,
will have his fore-flattened skull
and, gods willing, his fevered soul

back, buried finally and forever,
courtesy Ilwaco, Wash., Cemetery
Association. According to Meriweather,
head of the Chinook Council, "We
plan, for the event, a salmon bake;
we'll call it Chief Comcomly Day."

August 12. Slow birds tread the sun
above the open grave. The priest—
Baptist or Episcopalian,
pagan or seventh son of Crow—casts
a shadow too long for the time
of day. His eulogy turns on rhyme.

After salmon and wine, song birds
and a soft coastal rain begin.
The sun has sunk into the clouds.
Somewhere over against a mountain
a lone wolf lets out one wild howl.
The earnest sky begins to fall.

An unexpected hail. Hell
on dogs and birds. The sky can't hold
its wrath or praise long enough for all

45

this pomp and circumstance to mold
ancestral flesh onto his skull.
The eyes stay empty. The sky grows full.

Autobiography, Chapter XV: Agate Beach, California

Hanging on the edge of the world, I bat my eyes;
    the world stays firm, though this wild sea
    is a vision I'll never comprehend. Gull cries
    and breakers beating at my brain take the black
    beach like a storm of vampire wings. The great
    gray mound of water is total grave.

I came to see the sea, and now what I see is a crystal
    fear growing in my groin. This ocean is a lead
    lid on the coffin of the world, the sun a burning
    stake through the heart. I am diminished by the
    view. Dead eyes crowd the beach, agates clouded
    by the pale geography of time. Crab shells, sand
    dollars, a broken conch, and there near the last
    hard ebb: *my* bones.

Bones trembling still under the spell of the sea, I
    calm them, little white deaths that have known
    this west, in my entirely human hands. I throw
    them out to sea, finding that after all I still
    am grounded in sacrifice.

A suicide no doubt in less than twenty years, I'll
    not go easy, hoping all along something like
    this ill-named pacific shroud will toss me up
    again, as undead as each ninth wave and as
    inexplicable.

The Only Photograph of Quentin at Harvard

for Dan Rector

On the far left, at the edge,
a pair of hands holds
an open book.

At the right-hand bottom corner
a pair of shoes hangs
pegged to the wall,

the soles outward and soiled.
At the end of a word Shreve laces
his hands in his lap.

Central, across the checkered table,
Quentin counts the silence in his throat
below a half-

curtained bookcase. A mirror
reflects pictures pyramided
up a wall.

The one window is draped in white
gauze. Time is stilled
forever

in a hushed tone of sand.
The hands are about
to turn a page.

III
Ishmael

Myth is that which is taken for granted when thought begins.

Encyclopædia Britannica

My Father's House

i.

Below my father's house
are many meadows,

and beyond the meadows
the pawpaw trees

line the river banks.

I am alone here
where my father's voice

drifts, a small cloud,
in a sky too bright,

in a river far too clear.

ii.

What echoes there are
are here below

my father's house
among the pawpaw trees,

the shadowing leaves.

I am alone here,
stranger to words

and worlds I'll never know;
like the fruit of these trees

I grow soft

iii.

in summer wind,
remembering the firm

time, the sound of bells
in the meadows,

the lowing herds.

The dream ongoing,
the found past,

the one shadow
I always walk in,

my father's house.

Origin

Find a word
you haven't said or signed.

Farm it through
the very terraces of lung,
the steppes of eyes;
and watch a certain power grow,
an origin, a stem.

For there is a chemistry
to words:

how, for instance,
the saliva rises
to the tongue
as the word forms
like a cake
midthroat;

how, too,
the teeth grow
sharp
as the word
falls from the lips
like a green apple.

Molecular
as helix or hell,
words hold together even

stuff the deaf-mute's made of:
a tree of fingers,
a lace of flesh.

The Good Dark

East of the house
the frogs on the pond
prime the clouds
with thunder
under windy cattails.

The whole sky
boils black
as gunpowder
in the summer roll
of drums.

The rabbits
out of your garden
dive into little houses
under the grass,

and, surely, like you
gather the good dark
of home
about them
and sing
in the bombardment
of rain.

Tonight the Moon

for Carolyn

Tonight the moon comes red,
climbs on the earth's turning,
fades toward the white reflection
of your eyes.

Love, this night
is a night for holding the moon
like a fragile glass of wine.

I will take your white arms
as the moon claims our skin.

Inside my bones the marrow
maps the vintage sky.

I feel, Love, I feel
our passing as the moon passes,

and I will hold you, Love,
all the moons our bodies
complete themselves into,
into the final cast of moon.

Autobiography, Chapter XIII: Ghost Train, the Dream

For years that train drove every night, and its low
    dirge of steam filled the wind with a song
    beginning way beyond my eyes.

Always far off north of home, where the bottomlands
    were heavy with two slow rivers, where the cane-
    brakes splayed away into the weeping woman's slough,
    the distant roar of fire and steel drummed me nightly
    into dream.

I was cadenced by that dark engine off the edge of
    night into the dream of a drowned son, and am
    cadenced still.

For when the wind rises nights I cannot sleep, there's
    a certain droning in the air that wakes my bones:

I see the black hulk looming through the dark, its
    drivers pounding black smoke white against the
    weeping woman's moon,

and still I am lifted from myself and wailed away over
    dark water like some other mother's son.

After Dreams

for Carolyn

In dreams
I have flown
into myself,
through lands
heavy with
the lead
of nights
of no moon.

Soon now
I shall settle
softly down
like the down
of goslings
in no wind.

I shall pillow
my head with
your soft form
and wake in
the high blue
air of morning.

The Ghost's Story

What I wanted to do was only this:
touch the tender nape of your neck.

You moved away, never knowing me.
My hand is suspended in the light air,

still, of your passing. Your aura
holds my fingers in light repose,

the soft, gray air of morning framing
the bones, the flesh, in a pale wash

of blue, like the photo of a hand
that was never really there at all.

After a Postcard from Stryk in Japan

Lucien, all
the green river,
falling
green beneath
the green bridge,

all
the green houses,
their windows
opening light
onto the river

falling
now beyond
the green bridge
into the green sky,

and now
          all
               quiet
the green night blossoms.

Autobiography, Chapter XII: Hearing Montana

for Bob Conley

The distance drums your words into my ears; it's good
    to hear your voice backed by the force of snow.

I speak of things small enough to ride the wires and
    the Dakota winds. I try to find a certain power of
    words to make the distance thin.

And growing in my ears are the sounds I think we know:
    the flight of low geese, the awesome scream of
    owls, the sudden fall of skree.

I name these things with my weaker words, but feel a
    need to chant until the magic of my voice
    strikes me dumb as stone.

Words are sacred, friend, you remind me once again.
    I hear the cadence dancing on the wires and
    some other voices dimly cutting in

humming the weather, ways to know the snow, something
    with love in it, god knows what, as if these
    other voices are also somehow dimly you.

In Rudolph's Cave

In the cave
Rudolph found,
the walls hug
you like skin.
You fall
like a bucket
down vertical
stone and el east
into a devil's wedge
toward dark morning.
When finally
you crawfish
back, stand
and look
into the well
you must climb,
the amazement
in your mouth
is blinding.
There at
the bottom
of the shaft
into sky,
there, there,
on the still
blue surface
is one
pinpoint
of white.

Autobiography, Chapter III: Nearing El Paso

Into the brown sundown, we are free-falling, the bus
      sinking toward an illimitable offing of dusk,
      down, down with the sun.

Setting out is like this: you must acknowledge the horizon
      and count the hills you have to count.

Dream is part of it: you become that which you see, grow
      wise as stones, talk crow with birds.

And it all makes sense, even the salt wind off the blank
      face of Guadeloupe.

Everything is new, strange: you know it, it knows you.

Dog Days 1978

An affliction so general you find no name
to cover the pain: dog days in Missouri, same
low dull sky, the repetitive gray that clouds
every window, every pond, the very clods

in fields that die into a memory of autumn.
Dog days linger. The fire of frost to come
hardly attracts you at all, at all, so strong
is desire coursing your blood, in this long

time. Daily you look for words, but what you
always see is the cryptic flight of blue-
black birds against the gray, the invisible
script you are never fast enough or able

to read. And so. And so the days hang above
you, meaningless as the adolescent love
among the weathering stalks of corn. You mourn
these days, and every day you end with pain,

with desire swollen within that will pass
only with the season, the first death of grass,
of the stalks of corn, among which the farm girl names
her quick pain and the boy knows the power in his name.

One for Grand Ronde, Oregon

"I gave them fire . . . , blind hope."
—Aeschylus, *Prometheus Bound*

Ghosts of dead loggers haunt the night
where General Sheridan drove the light
into the last warring tribes. Grand Ronde
lies lead under the hoot-owl moon.

Indians and loggers die here still.
Years ago Big Moose drank his fill
of rotgut, told it like it was,
told them all to go to hell because

they were. The mountain called him up,
shook his senses clean, and let him jump.
Others still can hear his dark call
the nights the sky begins to fall.

No one has the guts to say where's hope.
Crow's a poor savior anymore. Croak
and feathers made the night. But now
what's left? The flayed god and the scowl

on the face of Spirit Mountain. The moon
is never right: the blood's too soon
for sacrifice and the constant rain
pounds like a wedge into the brain.

There's not one soul left in this town
who does not try to pray the frown
off the stone face the mountain's made
of: give us this day, god knows we've paid.

Autobiography, Chapter XVIII:
Camp in the Dead of Summer

The low sky settles lower on the trees, a dusk as humid
and salt as equatorial wind. There is no wind to
trade for rain. The limbs lash your face. You count
yourself, among the sweating blessed, a pilgrim
through the heavy green: gnarled oaks and witch
hazel, those silent screams, armed with arrows
pointing ways. The lost parent guided to his own
true son, bivouacked in a wilderness you would
not have him lose or leave for love nor honey of
a civilizing kiss. It's hell these summer days,
this treading air to stay alive as far as any camp.

You could die here without tears or sweat enough to keep
you cool. Lack of wind is wrong. Something is lying
ill at ease on land. The last night's retreat, and
you face the flags, absent among the scouts in stiff
salute. It's hard to face the fire and your son's
cloudless eyes. What you have lost is also his to lose.
You dread obituaries, wonder how you ever lived as
innocent and wild as the weathering stone his fire
is backed by. You long for home, that sanctuary of
loss. You listen with your humming ears to his rare
enthusiastic woe: his tale of trials among the caves

and other rituals he was honored in. All his badges are
stitched in green thread: an innocence of rage and
insects. You cannot tell him once you touched a
nesting hawk, slept alone seven nights under a canopy
of cracking trees, falling stars, that wild-woman
moon gone mad. A vision hard to call back now that

the earth turns and the world is real with dollars
and horse sense. You misremember most bad dreams:
to stay alive you have to sing and lie. His words
pass into your eyes. Or maybe it's sweat that stings.
The words move in, and night moves west with your
life. You anticipate a descending wind. You shake
his hand scoutwise. It's dry and flesh, the squeeze
a kiss of bones. You say goodbye the best you can,
tell him to obey the lay of land and time. You
mean it the way you think you lived and daily died.

Lost in Sulphur Canyons

All the stones
unturned say
you are alone.

Not even a sun
cracks
the lead sky.

The deer
you thought
you tracked
has never known
the stones
you step on.

Stone by stone
you follow
the small water
down through
sulphur springs
rank as the fear
you try not
to taste.

For such descent
as this, you need
a guide, someone
to lean a word
or curse on.

Only the stones
know your breath
is wrong.

An absence
of wind grays
the pines
and your hair.

You stoop
to drink
your face.

The sweet, white
bite of water
leaves you stunned.

You smile to see
a face pale
against the sky,
a smile
you never knew
was there at all.

With all the hell
of sulphur and pitch
you know somehow
you couldn't be
happier, lost
as a stray dog
among the stones.

Autobiography, Chapter IX: Leaving, Again

You've got to leave this land again before it hurts
    you into a sin the years will not ease: a constant
    fear swells in your groin, and there's a singing
    in the trees your blood wants to beat time to.

Easy it would be to stay and dream, to walk-wolf these
    woods and fields, to play what you've always been
    and are afraid to be. You know there's a crescendo
    building in your blood, a raging conquistador, wild
    sailor, part pilgrim looking for a mecca he'll never
    find. Or find and lose and find again.

Dreams you once had in a bad time come back to haunt
    your ears: sounds of music too sensual for light
    drum dark in the soft trees, and the leaves begin
    again to dance and shapes take form, lovely and
    green.

You see the muddy river clear, sirens naked on its banks.
    A wild urge silent on their lips tells you plain this
    land will always sing you back, quick with dream, your
    hands always poised for overture.

The Iowa Sequence

i. Waterloo

Stranger to
the moated center,
I try to mold
my face native.
Full of trees,
my eyes are quick
to show the lie.
The poet I came
to hear beats time
to traffic as foreign
as my mind.
I find no common ground.
The artificial lake,
its wind and waves,
are distance
I cannot bridge.
His words do not
walk water.

ii. Marshalltown

Christ would like
hanging here:
the sky portends
earthquake.
There's a heavy air
at noon, thick as oil,
entombed thunder from
mountains glaciered

flat and black.
Jean Seberg's hometown
and bête noire, a town
to leave your sins in,
from where every road
goes up.

iii. Muscatine

Home of mustard and melons,
cradle of rats and river,
your façades speak
of better times, windows
cracked, blued brittle
by this awful wind.
Your one fat street,
a tongue black with names
old as vinegar,
crosses your one steepled hill
and falls straight
into the Mississippi.

iv. Mason City

The museum here
preserves the heart
of Iowa: an unfinished
eighteenth-century portrait
details a face in
white, the features
as serene as death mask.
Nothing is complete
except the face, the face:
all else a shroud of lines.

v. Nora Springs

They say Indians
washed away their sins
here; that's why
the river stinks.
The fish I catch
are cancerous and black.
I haven't seen
the sun in weeks.
The river does not run.
There's a general
sinking of the ground.
I think I hear
the natives praying.

Autobiography, Chapter XI: Prelude to Writing

I am dreaming. I am sitting here dreaming. It is raining
and a good time for dreaming. I do not know whether
the poetry will come today. If it does, I will be
ready for it.

I think it is going to come soon. There was an image of a
footbridge a moment's eye ago, and a river under it.
The water was still with a scum on it, and what looked
like, from that distance, a paper boat. It could have
been a paper sack. But that doesn't matter. Sack or
boat.

*   *   *

A limestone bluff to the north. I think I see a cave, wild
flowers at the mouth. Steps leading down from the top.
I walk down them. Someone has lived in this place. In
powdered stone, the soft imprint of a thigh. Ants trail
across the dunes.

Strange how the wind writes on water. The wind carries the
scum away, and the sky floats by the mouth of the cave.
Someone is looking out across the river. It must be me,
but I do not know the eyes. They are a long way back,
and they see only the reflection on the water, not the
water itself. They are looking at the falling sky.

*   *   *

The water is suddenly white with geese, which see something
startling. The geese do not fly; they paddle dumb and
careful circles around one another, timing each stroke

with the certainty of flight. I am sure of one thing:
they want to know what it is amazes them before they
try the heavy sky.

*   *   *

On the bridge, someone has left a grandfather's clock. Its
    face is peeling in the rain, and the short hand is
    missing. I turn the key: there is an odd sound, like
    sunlight striking leaves, or kisses in dark old doorways.
    Something is going to start in a minute if I keep turning
    the key.

10-4-76
Mason City, Iowa

Memoirs of a Catskinner

We downed the cathedral
with ball and crane.
I confessed just once
to a flying saint,
then swore silence
in the nauseous dust.

All day I dreamed
quiet prairies, wild
chicory and coneflowers.

Splinters
from stained glass
and falling gargoyles
shrouded my green glasses,
and Lord
the noise: the yellow cat
knocking pews
seven ways to Sunday.

I consecrated meadows
in my head,
counted gopher holes.

The foreman jumped my ass
at lunch for backtracking
onto the street: Keep it
on holy ground, he said.
I genuflected.
He twirled the masonic ring,
third finger, right hand.

Toward sundown
I took the altar
into my blade
and fishes fell.

O Lord, I yelled
in the bursting air,
let my eardrums fail
forever
in some other world.

I herded sheep
through red clover
and silent wind,
columns of steady air.

I dozed into the vacant crypt,
and prayed:
Let them dig my grave
by hand
O Lord.

On the Bridge at Fourche Maline River

Forty feet below, the water stands as dull
as dog days. No movement toward the lake
ten snaking miles away. You stand here full
of hope you have always been told to have,
with no regard for the ruined years, those rabid
foxes at your heels.

                        You stop here whenever
you have the time. The river's pull is strong.
The dark water, too thick and slow to reflect
anything outside itself, sends a constant song.
Worlds away you always know the river
is your home. You've never seen the river
run toward its sea. Yet it moves at the touch
when you take time to go down, lay your hands
on the warm river, and speak to the current
that flows into and through your blood.

                                        It has
been years since you swam this muddy stream
and, bearing a rock for ballast, walked the bottom
straight across, bank to bank, in the longest breath
you ever held. Time and time again, as now,
you dream that walk. This time it's real. You leave
your clothes flapping on the rail and jump, wide,
into the warm water and feel the river
bottom wrap a gentle skin about your feet.
As you break upward for breath, you taste
the sweet meat of earth the river is made of,
and you remember the earth and that you are home.

The Last Chance

The myna bird speaks
of love. His whistle
cuts into the bone
ears of a whitetail's
head stuffed above
the bar.

Fifty miles the county's
dry. You stop here
to tell yourself
go home, but hear
the black experience
of a goddamned bird

whose hello sucks
at the marrow
of your bones.
You wonder how a soul
can pass from
his beak and break

upon your face, split
the whiskers you grew
to be wise in. You wonder
at his avalanche of words,
the last drink you took,
the dance on your skin

you can't beat time to.
You wonder, but you
do not ask. You

listen hard with
your cracking eyes.
He asks about your life.

You tell him lies
while he prunes
a feather, lets it drop.
Your life is sour
in the glass. Crow
made the earth and all

things therein, brought fire.
This bird's a ghost
you tell your sins.
Nobody is listening.
Outside, the sun falls
into the brittle grass.

IV
Night Falls, Ritual and Fast

After everything ends
and even while the story goes on
I accept all that is left over.

WILLIAM STAFFORD
"The Whole Story"

Year's End 1977

"One must have a mind of winter."
—Wallace Stevens

The moon lies to the bedded snow:
the all-night dawn is as good as day.
This is the mind of winter that you have come to know.

All night long you have looked for the right
words to rid your mind of all the day
in order to see the nothing that is of a winter's night.

The silence upon the fields holds you
in its steady light, and your eyes
become the nothing of light you try to see clearly through.

The vision blurs in blowing snow:
zodiacs of flake and wind take
orbit in your mind, and something final begins to grow,

the long year's end. You cannot stay
blank as winterscape and survive
the lesson of snow, the igloo of ice that domes the winter's day.

All that is told in the nothing that is
escapes you in the breath you take,
but breathe you will this winter's night the nothing that surely is.

Winter Pastoral

The tracks in snow cut the hill in half,
and the hunter draws his bow. A bath
of light, shuddered from the frozen moon,
washes his shoulders white, gathers
the shadows tightly as a loom.

His hands are constantly in place.
A rapid sound of broken ice
cracks the timber on the hill,
then recedes with the cautious pace
of animals weaving past a kill.

And now the hunter's moon is down.
The snow is dark where the tracks wound
the fading light. The silence of snow,
the soft thread, once again is spun
by the breath of stars the hunter knows.

For one thing, you can believe it:
the skin chewed soft enough to wear,
the bones hewn hard as a totem
from hemlock. It's a kind of scare-

crow that will follow you home nights.
You've seen it ragged against a field,
but you seldom think, at the time,
to get there it had to walk through hell.

Midwest Midwinter

i.

You know it's true the sky has fallen:
a blue has settled upon the ground
and gray fields grow solid overhead.
Points of light, thousands, break behind your eyes.
A nova whirls about your nose.
Your mind implodes, black hole in space,
and draws all sound and sense
to a center you never want to be.

ii.

The hard gravity of ice holds you down.
Days like this it's hard to move.
Landscape is constantly the same.
You envy Venezuelans the warmer world.
You've bottomed out at 10 below.
A jungle of snow is vining up
the day. Night falls, ritual and fast.

iii.

Even dreams are static. The frozen womb
you crawl into each night holds you
as fast as amber the arachnid's legs.
Promethean to the night, you count
the links in chains, wonder at what
secret you can possibly possess.

Sounds you hear hang in old doorways
like the severed lips of liars, false
to the last bitter bite of that cold steel.
The sharp midwinter wind cuts a steady moan,
one you ride on across the reluctant moon.

Autobiography, Chapter II: Setting Out

The green blurs across your eyes. It is May, you remember, and you
   are leaving at last. Oklahoma! The window of the bus you look
   out of throws your shadow into the trees: even the shadow is
   green. You try to save your face. You swear you'll be a seasoned
   tenderfoot.

The land swells and rolls, then spreads out like the night toward
   Oklahoma City, where you know you'll change for El Paso and
   the Southwest to cross the desert Coronado knew all the way to
   an ocean you cannot yet dream. You will eat the desert and the
   high loneliness of the buttes: this is your dream, the going.
   You will consume the land; it will course your veins. You will
   be in and of the land.

The City, widest town on earth, is barely limited by the arch of sky.
   Miles there is nothing but neon and hard sin. The City hits your
   face with the smell of hot tar, an acid eating at your eyes. Two
   infernal hours and you leave, frightened and glad the
       Greyhound
   cuts the night clean as lightning. Too many ghosts are loping at
   your heels, but you know you are running straight to what you
   were born for.

Into the night, dead night now, finally free of neon and breaking
   shadows, you feel yourself flowing on some river you can't yet
   name, but it does not matter. What matters is that you know
   you are going and the going is good.

The Exact Center of the World

The owl among the trees screaming
like a mad mother's ghost is gone.
The mound of the guarding owl has sunk,
its skull nearly level with the ground.
The stones move in. A new forest
in twisted form crawls to the place
you found hard midnight at fifteen:
heard the screech owl scream, the moon fall,
and the breaking of ancestral bones.

Here you knew a first real fear and ran
past the second wind you never felt.
Dark times. But now the moon is back
and your eyes clear in the chalk of night.
Now you know all the ghosts are dead,
except the one never laid to rest:
this mound in this clearing is the exact
center of the world. All things move round
it. And here sundown explains nothing.

Against Metempsychosis &c.

Now that I am old and uneasy under the weathering trees
    and see time in the light of the fog
snaking among branches, hollows, low places in the earth,
the days slough off themselves and from themselves and all
    disease
is a floundering of the mind to comprehend at last the first
    rule of rot: that the melding logs

underfoot are hostel and hotel for claw, fang, tooth, nail.
    And yet I cannot see the rhyme
at the end of the log, the metrics that make the ebb and flow
of wood flesh turn fowl or field right in the diffused pale
aura of each winding day. That days should ever snow
    themselves green with a riddling mime

is not to be I know. Thanks to the wobbling earth seasons
    hold: gnats bite, die, things work out. What
I do see is little more than ant, a refusal to mourn
something I can never accept, a passing. Few reasons,
and fewer still, do me now that I am old, stiff as horn,
    untidy, subject to bugs, their snouts

always out. I'm unreasonable clay. I will not change nor see
    beauty in anything as obscene as
a passing day. Age, easily attainable, sees me now
flounder, fish out of water, in a world (forever knee-
deep at least) of slip not of my making but mine, and though
    fired through with a mind as flaked as

vintage pots, I'm lucky to make mud pies in this slow time
    that anyone will believe in,

much less flaunt with praise. Of course I am much bothered by
    loss:
insipid verse I can't recall, taxes paid, a traffic fine,
a wife, two kids in school who can't do math, or dental floss
    biting in my gums. All this, then

some nut comes philosophizing on rot, the great skein of life.
    Just what I need certainly is not
a dissertation on rot. Give me the bad mind that boils
in anger against rot, fever between the eyes, tempered knife
blade in the temple. In short, mine. Little though it is, it coils,
    will spring, be sprung (who cares?), not rot.

Autobiography, Chapter XIX:
For Andrew Grossbardt, in Memoriam

The slow summer falls about us like manna, sustenance
    we do not understand. The August moon wanes toward
    harvest here in the heavy heart of America, where
    once you timed your words.

Abstractions warp my tongue: I taste hot iron whenever
    I try to reason why *that* last act. My thirst was
    yours, yours mine, you taught me that. Now in this
    quiet time I lean toward the night to try to hear
    the echoes of a song, music you lived by, words
    and words alone.

Whatever siren's call you heard before you leaped into
    the storied night, my friend, is your last once
    upon a time. You must have fathomed deep, tied
    as you were to words, to loose the bounds we all laid
    round you daily and unaware.

The silence that is your death I do not take lightly.
    It passes as the wind passes, as the rays of the
    sun shimmer into the sea, as the seasons endlessly
    roll round earth—with circumstance.

Autobiography, Chapter IV: The Mirage

Out of Yuma and heading west, you feel the lift of air: a thermal
dares you to try your wings.

There is a dance of heat way down the road, a swaying atmosphere,
and suddenly you see the dance turn clear as ice, and above
the ice a mountain that is not there.

A floating island and a cold inland sea: too much for the mind
to take in such a heat. You bat your eyes and caves of wind
take form. The island undulates in dance. You think you see
a ship.

The desert dips, and your mind is slow to follow your body down.
Heading toward the end of sky, the bus realizes the road. You
see the mirage with another set of eyes. You see the mountain
real as the wind against the window you count your own eyes in.

Wild Horse Hollow

The sound of drums is the distance
in your ears. Stones swell these hills,
and the hogbacks hunker under the honing
moon as if the land fears a deadly siege
of night. The moon turns your hands
gunmetal gray: the muzzle of your wrist
begins to glow, and why you came grows
vague under a shooting star. You stoop
to taste the snowy earth and night
you know you'll never be able to dream.
A sudden shadow strafes your eyes.
You flinch, and your quick finger
triggers into the forked stick you hold.
The wild horses you swear you know once
were here have left no sign, not one
trail across stone to hang a legend on.

Autobiography, Chapter V: Ghost Town

Boards the shape of shadows, windows blued by the awful
   sun, the black hollow of gone doors, and always the
   constant sound of wind.

You try to take this absent town in one bound of soul,
   afraid you'll stumble on the derelict years only
   the headstones name.

You fail. The mind finds a stop: a rainbow in broken
   glass, a stream of dust in the washed-out street,
   footsteps you can't possibly hear.

The half saloon bangs its half a door the wind walks
   through. Night falls like hail, down with the
   thirsting hills.

You spread your blankets before the blank eyes of the
   town and lie in wait, a poor thief, for the permanence
   of stars. Inside your throat hangs a silence: there
   are no words, no words.

Autobiography, Chapter VIII: At the Sand Fields

Sand shifts under your feet as though it flows toward some silent,
    dangerous sea: sand, weeds, and an ebb and flow of a sun
    that flails your back red.

A lone hawk circles high, a question of territory in his sharp cry;
    a desolation burns at the marrow of your bones.

You have pirated these fields of artifacts for as long as you can
    remember, but the numbered bones have yet to make a man, or
    even yet a single limb.

You have not learned the hawk's song.

Still you run the swells of these fields looking for survivors,
    the perfect stone, the last jigsaw bone.

The hawk cries again, and the sky flags piece by piece down into
    your face, and your eyes crack with the sound of broken weeds.

Loving the Distant Nude

She is lying freely among the dunes,
her breasts, her thighs, slow and undulating,
like the oceanic swells beyond the dunes.

The subtle flesh and the rise and fall of dunes
rebuff all fact and logic of the day:
I mold my own body into the dunes.

The distance is growing dark between the dunes.
Her perfect thighs are wedded to the secret
night I place us in. The air brushes the dunes:

flaws dissolve in the black and white the dunes
become in full-moon light. Distant, we are
engaged in an act of love, like dunes on dunes;

distant, yet wholly one, each knowing the dunes
hold the other's eyes, the other's body.
The touch is more real, the distance bridged by dunes.

The Family Plot

They tried to get me, one and all,
to go to church, sit in the front-row
pew, pray. I feigned indifference to
God and man. Oh, secretly though
I was awed by the graveyard through
which I ran when moon and owl

both were dark and I late for home.
Only the lateness of the hour
made me a boy brave enough then
to take the shortcut through flowers,
stone slabs of unacknowledged sin,
the *Requiescat In Pace* blown

in the unrelenting wind. I knew
the stones that lined the path by heart,
not by head, and was struck, changed
by windy death each time the start
of night bird or stalking beast ranged
up the length of spine and through

my hair. Dead uncles, aunts, deacons,
all spelled death and I would have none
of that. Father, mother, brother,
sister, cousins, all woebegone
because they knew how much I'd rather
sing hillbilly than their true songs.

I hid my crazy fear of death
to all except the limbo souls
along the path I'd sometimes take:

only the shades could know my palms
were cold from more than cold, the ache
of aging in my living breath.

Tornado

I am running; it is night,
I run toward the light.

Dark cuts through me like whiskey.

The light comes from the house.

The house is running; it is still night.
The house runs toward the light.

Dark cuts through the house like whiskey.

The light comes from me.

Stopping on Kiamichi Mountain

Antlers ten miles. You read the sign shot full
of holes. Everything you see is at least
half lie. You gun the Mustang and the engine
pings. Bullets ricochet off your head.
Sulphur Spring the arrow points, and you stop
to learn again the canyon hard below
is home to snakes and tarantulas as fierce
as fire in jack pines.

                 Nothing is what
it seems. The cliché clogs; you try to shift
your mind. You idle down the trail, half
aware there's little sign of game and the wind
is still. The spring is down, a trickle, crusted
with raw sulphur that smells of hell and crap.
The sound of thunder breaks the hills in half.
You had forgotten the deadly still is always
prelude to a wind that rattlers will even
leave their skins to flee.

                 The thunder jars
you hard into yourself, the land. The sound
of home. God knows you know the tornado's
wake will suck your sins right out your guts.
The trees shake in the first wave of the wind.
Darkness descends like a hawk on prey.

                    Antlers
and you'll find yourself in that other home
away from home. The Buckhorn and three-two

beer. You feel you've earned a drunk, one that
will cauterize your guts and put a handle
on the wind.

You head the Mustang straight into
the dark and pray the only times you ever
do that you know the wind by Indian name.

Autobiography, Chapter XLII:
Three Days in Louisville

Everything is the cause of itself.
Ralph Waldo Emerson

i.

Coming down into an air brown as whiskey, the plane
    drops onto the strip like a practiced crow ready
    for another's kill, talons wild for dead game.

This fierce town will hold you three days running:
    the nervous prance that cracks your bones tells
    you plain there's nothing sure about sure things.

You count your chances for survival slim; this is no
    town for poets: the weather is never right, the
    air a constant sour mash and scream.

The city sprawls like a gutted horse, and the taxi
    you take can't even offer tours, the hotel so
    cold it smells of juniper and gin.

In East St. Louis this morning a stable burned;
    the horses screaming in their stalls, a total
    loss; and now you burn, wild mares beating in
    your brain, but you're no hero, barely sane.

You will read your poems to whoever is there or to
    the night; you will read something with hoofs
    in it, something with hands, something in the
    saddle to ride mankind.

You eat Italian with your friends, who have driven a thousand
    miles, weathered well through the gangstered middle of this
    land, are green for poetry and bourbon on the rocks.

The horses in your head are pulling at the reins, anxious for
    the race they cannot run; a heavy smell of char stings
    your eyes, the sight of steak singed and bloody turns
    you cold.

There is no muse to pull a poem out of this pot; your fat
    friend across your plate plays Petrarchian with his words,
    the bad sonnet falling from his mouth like sauce.

When you were young, the horses in the meadows danced
    and the grooming wind greened their eyes and the sun
    filled their hoofs with fire.

Now the horses die, die, and the violent sky cracks with
    the thunder of stampede, gods gone crazy in the whiskey
    dark.

Hands above your head to keep your vision clear, you rush
    the car, stagger in mid-air: half buried in the rainy
    pavement at your feet is a spent cartridge of a Smith
    and Wesson .45.

iii.

The muraled walls are big with horses' heads; paddocks
    and colonels are cornering at every turn you make.

You enter the Poetry Room at half-lope, late, your bones
    popping like pistols at the track. Three days in

Louisville and your brain ferments a race you swore
you'd never see: you dream pasterns broken, nostrils
flared, a bullet between the eyes.

You loose your poems and the words run out, but you can't
   loose the horses in your head: in Tennessee, or somewhere
   down from here, they wrap the pasterns tight in wire
   and the Walking Horse learns his name dancing three-
   quarter time.

You've come to dread the afterwards, the taking stock that
   follows poems that's supposed to help you tighten up
   the pace. You know it's hard to drop a line or life.
   Always too much at stake.

The bourbon you finally allow yourself in bed is pure flame.
   You take it like you take the lie of sunny weather on
   TV. Agape. On the nightstand a phonebook and a Gideon
   lie neck to neck.

Self-Portrait

I am
before
a window.

A rain falls,
a leaf falls.

Behind me
a door closes.

Autobiography: Last Chapter

Coming in again, you know the town by boards it makes eyes
    touch, summer shirtsleeves worn long, heavy hats pulled
    down.

Always the wind stinks.

The woman you loved summers ago sits pale as bleached stones,
    her husband mad, their house a heap of broken bones.

The sky lies faded denim above your cousin's store; the false-
    front from another age, dogeared as a tinhorn's wild
    joker, can't reflect your past in its cracked eye.

You want to cry, but know the sun turns tears to salt before
    they break from lids in this desperate town, where the
    only hope is a brittle Baptist bell banging sometimes
    Sundays.

You touch the woman by your side and want to explain the lack
    of paint away, but don't: she knows you are running back
    into yourself.

Poetry from Illinois